Maths Age 5-6

Melissa Blackwood, Liz Dawson & Stephen Monaghan

In a strange place, not too far from here, lives a scare of monsters.

A 'scare' is what some people call a group of monsters, but these monsters are really very friendly once you get to know them.

They are a curious bunch – they look very unusual, but they are quite like you and me, and they love learning new things and having fun.

In this book you will go on a learning journey with the monsters and you are sure to have lots of fun along the way.

Do not forget to visit our website to find out more about all the monsters and to send us photos of you in your monster mask or the monsters that you draw and make!

Contents

- 2 Numbers and Number Words
- 4 Place Value
- 6 More Place Value
- 7 Number Patterns
- 8 Addition
- 10 Subtraction
- 12 Multiplication and Division
- 14 Monster Challenge 1
- 16 Fun Fractions
- 18 2-Dimensional (2-D) Shapes
- 20 3-Dimensional (3-D) Shapes
- 22 Measuring
- 24 What is the Time, Poggo?
- 26 Data Handling
- 28 Monster Challenge 2
- 30 Answers
- 32 Monster Match

Numbers and Number Words

Mum has written a shopping list. Poggo has noticed that Mum has used a mixture of numbers and number words in the list.

Mum explains that they can be written as numbers or words but mean the same thing.

> two monster muffins
> 6 monster bites
> one bottle of Monster Fizz Drink

1 Mum wants to test Poggo about the names of numbers. Point at the number and say the correct name for each one.

0, 6, 10, 5, 15, 19

1, 16, 3, 11, 4

9, 13, 2, 17, 8, 18

20, 7, 12, 14

2 Help Poggo to match up the number with the number word by drawing a line.

sixteen		20	2		eight
fifteen		0	10		nineteen
twenty		16	5		twelve
three		4	12		thirteen
eighteen		15	19		five
zero		3	8		two
four		18	13		ten

Fun Zone!

Here is a game that you can make and play with friends and family.

What a great game!
You can now find and colour **Shape 1** on the Monster Match page!

Number Snap Game

You will need 21 small squares of yellow card, 21 small squares of green card, a pen and a partner to play with.
Ask an adult to help when needed.

1. Write each number between 0 and 20 on the yellow card squares. Then write the number words on the green cards.
2. Muddle the yellow and green cards separately and spread them out face down.
3. Take it in turns to turn over a yellow card and a green card to match the number and its number word.
4. If you get a match, keep the cards until the end of the game. If you do not find a match, place the cards face down again.
5. The winner is the person with the most cards.

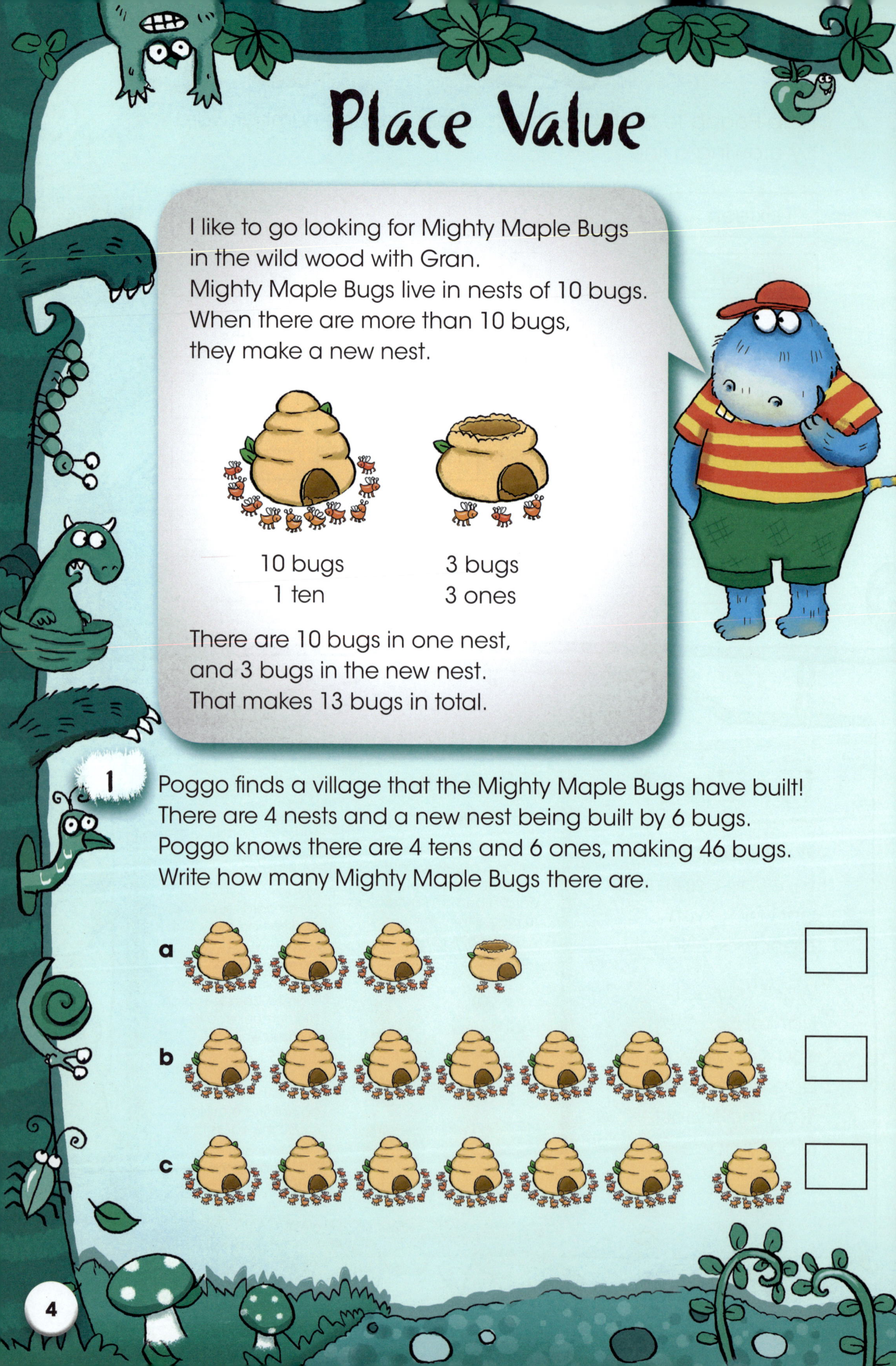

2 Help Poggo draw a picture of how many Mighty Maple Bugs he has seen.
The first one has been done for you.

a 34

b 27

c 52

Fun Zone!

Build your own monster den.

Great work! You can now find and colour **Shape 2** on the Monster Match page!

Monster Den

You will need some furniture (such as chairs) or a clothes airer and a large piece of fabric, such as a sheet or tablecloth.

Ask an adult to help when needed.
1. Find a clear space in your house.
2. Arrange the furniture or clothes airer so that you can crawl in between them and a wall.
3. Cover them with the fabric and hold it in place (you could use books or pegs).
4. Crawl into your den and have a monsterific time!

More Place Value

Poggo needs new skateboard wheels and goes to the skateboard shop. There are lots of baskets of wheels he can choose from.

Poggo knows that the basket with 43 wheels has the **most** wheels, because it is the biggest number.
The basket with the smallest number of wheels has the **least** number of wheels.

1 Circle the basket that has the **most** wheels.

2 Circle the basket with the **least** number of wheels.

Number Patterns

An **odd number** ends with 1, 3, 5, 7 or 9.

An **even number** ends with 0, 2, 4, 6 or 8.

1 Poggo is entering the skateboarding competition. The competing monsters put a competition number on their skateboards.
The monsters with odd numbers go first.

Colour in the skateboards with **odd** numbers.

7   23   11   30   59   8

2 Here is Poggo's final score.
Is it an **odd** or **even** number?

96

_____

Fun Zone!

Have fun doing some messy marble painting!

Well done! You can now find and colour **Shape 3** on the Monster Match page!

Messy Marble Painting

You will need poster paint, a paint tray, marbles and paper. Ask an adult to help when needed.

1. Put some paint into a tray.
2. Roll a marble in the paint so it is covered.
3. Put the marble on the paper, and tip the paper so the marble rolls around.
4. Use different colours to create a messy marble masterpiece.

Addition

The monsters are putting up some balloons for Nano's birthday party. Kora can see that they need to add some more balloons.
She checks how many they have already.

Adding means counting how many balloons there are **altogether**.
The **total** number is always bigger than the numbers you start with.
The **addition symbol** looks like **+**.

5   +   8   =   13

1 Count how many balloons there are altogether.

a

☐ + ☐ = ☐

b

☐ + ☐ = ☐

2 Kora has 25 party poppers and she buys 13 more.
She uses a number line to help her count how many
she has altogether.
25 + 13 = 38 party poppers **altogether**.

2 3 4 5 6 7 8 9 10 11 12 13 14 15 16 17 18 19 20 21 22 23 24 25 26 27 28 29 30 31 32 33 34 35 36 37 38 39 40 41 42

Use the above number line to add:

a 23 + 14 = ☐   d 11 + 17 = ☐

b 29 + 3 = ☐   e 32 + 9 = ☐

c   7 + 23 = ☐   f 23 + 2 = ☐

3 Kora now needs to put the cups out ready for the drinks.
She puts out 23 cups for the children and 12 cups for the adults.
How many cups are there altogether?
Write a number sentence to show how you have worked it out.
You could use the number line above to help you.

Fun Zone!

Make a monster mask.

Excellent work! You can now find and colour **Shape 4** on the Monster Match page!

Monster Mask

You will need a paper plate, paint or felt tips, string, scissors and glue. Ask an adult to help when needed.

1 Draw a monster face on the plate.
2 Get an adult to help you cut out eye and mouth holes.
3 Decorate the plate using lots of different colours in a monster pattern.
4 Put one hole at each side of the plate.
5 Thread the string through.
6 Tie the string around the back of your head, and roar like a monster.

Subtraction

When Litmus points his 'Super Subtractor' at something, it makes the object disappear. Litmus tests it by pointing it at one of his pencils.

The **subtraction symbol** looks like **–**.

5 – 1 = 4

Now Litmus uses his 'Super Subtractor' on 34 test tubes and makes 11 disappear. He starts at 34 on a **number line** and counts back to work out how many test tubes are left.

34 – 11 = 23

1 Work out how many pencils are left.

a ☐ – ☐ = ☐

b ☐ – ☐ = ☐

2 Help Litmus work out how many test tubes are left after the 'Super Subtractor' has made some disappear. Use the number line to help you.

```
|||||||||||||||||||||||||||||||||||||||
12 13 14 15 16 17 18 19 20 21 22 23 24 25 26 27 28 29 30 31 32 33 34 35 36 37 38 39 40 41 42 43 44 45 46 47 48 49 50
```

a 34 − 17 = ☐   d 16 − 4 = ☐

b 49 − 18 = ☐   e 50 − 25 = ☐

c 28 − 12 = ☐   f 49 − 19 = ☐

3 Litmus had 37 ingredients for new experiments. The 'Super Subtractor' has made 18 disappear. Write a number sentence to show how many are left. Use the number line above to help you.

☐

Fun Zone!

Have fun going on a bug hunt!

Monsterific! You can now find and colour **Shape 5** on the Monster Match page!

Bug Hunt

You will need a pad of paper and a pen or pencil.
Ask an adult to help when needed.

1 Go outside and see how many bugs you can find.
2 Remember to look under rocks, bushes and sticks.
3 Record the bugs that you find on your piece of paper. How many different bugs can you find?
4 Remember to put the bugs back where you found them.
5 Now wash your hands.

Multiplication and Division

Poggo is counting how many gloves Kora has altogether.
He can add them one at a time but he can also count in 2s.
This is called **repeated addition**.

Kora has 4 gloves and Poggo wants to know how many fingers the yellow gloves have altogether.
There are **5** fingers on each glove so he groups them into 5s.
He uses repeated addition to find the answer.
Kora has **10** fingers altogether.

Poggo is sharing his Monster Sports Cards with Fizz.
When objects are shared out equally, this is called **dividing**.
Poggo has **12** cards and shares them equally.

Now Poggo and Fizz both have **6 each**.

1 Count the number of gloves altogether using repeated addition. Remember to circle each group of 2.

a There are ☐ gloves altogether.

b There are ☐ gloves altogether.

2 Count the number of fingers altogether using repeated addition.

a 🖐️🖐️🖐️🖐️🖐️

There are ☐ fingers altogether.

b 🖐️🖐️🖐️🖐️🖐️🖐️🖐️🖐️🖐️

There are ☐ fingers altogether.

3 Poggo has been asked by Mum to share more of his cards equally with Fizz. Draw the cards below.

a Share 10 cards.

Poggo   Fizz

b Share 8 cards.

Poggo   Fizz

Fun Zone!

Create your own monster gloves.

Fantastic! You can now find and colour **Shape 6** on the Monster Match page!

Monster Gloves

You will need an old pair of gloves, scraps of felt or fabric, scissors and glue.

Ask an adult to help when needed.

1. Cut out small triangles from the fabric and glue these at the end of the fingers to make monster nails. They could be yellow, or have jagged edges!
2. Cut small pieces of fabric and glue these all over the backs of your gloves.
3. Now you have hairy, scary monster hands!

Monster Challenge 1

1 Match the word to the correct number.

2	twenty
18	two
11	nine
9	eighteen
20	eleven

2 Write down how many tens and ones each number has.

Number	Tens	Ones
43	4	3
12		
98		
76		
57		

3 Circle the number below that is the **biggest**.

a 18   24   9   c 35   1   99

b 89   10   16   d 53   34   78

4 Circle the number below that is the **smallest**.

a 89   55   23   c 67   89   42

b 53   73   5   d 52   72   12

5 Use the number line to answer the **addition** questions.

|||||||||||||||||||||||||||||||||||||||||
11 12 13 14 15 16 17 18 19 20 21 22 23 24 25 26 27 28 29 30 31 32 33 34 35 36 37 38 39 40 41 42 43 44 45 46 47 48 49 50

a 23 + 6 = ☐   c 11 + 22 = ☐

b 42 + 8 = ☐   d 32 + 12 = ☐

6 Use the number line to answer the **subtraction** problems.

|||||||||||||||||||||||||||||||||||||||||
15 16 17 18 19 20 21 22 23 24 25 26 27 28 29 30 31 32 33 34 35 36 37 38 39 40 41 42 43 44 45 46 47 48 49 50

a 48 − 6 = ☐   c 28 − 12 = ☐

b 34 − 3 = ☐   d 41 − 22 = ☐

7 Colour the **odd** numbers in blue and the **even** numbers in red.

1	2	3	4	5	6	7	8	9	10
11	12	13	14	15	16	17	18	19	20

8 Find the total number of mini-monsters by counting them in the groups they are in.

a   = ☐   b   = ☐

9 Share the monster coins equally between Fizz and Tizz.

Fizz   Tizz

Fun Fractions

Poggo and Tizz are sharing a monster cake.
Poggo explains that they should each have the same – that is called **half** and that makes it a 'fair share'.

One **half** has 1 part out of 2 shaded.

One **quarter** has 1 part out of 4 shaded.

Three-quarters has 3 parts out of 4 shaded.

Tizz now knows how to shade in one half, one quarter and three-quarters of a shape, but still does not know how to write them as a number.

The number is called a **fraction** and can be written like this:

One half: $\frac{1}{2}$ One quarter: $\frac{1}{4}$ Three-quarters: $\frac{3}{4}$

1   a Help Tizz colour half of each of the shapes below.

b Help Tizz colour one quarter of each shape.

2 Help Tizz to colour in the squares correctly.
Halves should be **blue**, **quarters red** and **three-quarters yellow**.
Be careful, because there are both fraction numbers and fractions of shapes in the grid!

$\frac{3}{4}$	▨ half	$\frac{1}{4}$	$\frac{3}{4}$	▨ three-quarters	$\frac{1}{2}$
▨ half	▨ quarter	$\frac{1}{2}$	$\frac{3}{4}$	▨ three-quarters	$\frac{1}{4}$
$\frac{3}{4}$	▨ half	$\frac{3}{4}$	$\frac{1}{4}$	$\frac{1}{2}$	$\frac{3}{4}$
$\frac{1}{4}$	▨ half	$\frac{3}{4}$	▨ half	$\frac{1}{2}$	▨ quarter
▨ quarter	$\frac{3}{4}$	$\frac{1}{4}$	▨ half	▨ three-quarters	$\frac{1}{2}$

Fun Zone!

Design a new flag that is split into either halves, quarters or three-quarters.

Well done! You can now find and colour **Shape 7** on the Monster Match page!

Family Flag

You will need a large piece of paper and felt-tip pens or colouring pencils.

Ask an adult to help when needed.

1. Divide your flag into sections so that each member of the family has a section. For example, if there are 4 people in your family, divide your flag into quarters.

2. Carefully draw and colour something to represent each family member in their section. For example, if your sister loves to roller skate, you could draw roller skates in her section and colour the background with her favourite colour.

3. Hang your finished flag near your front door.

2-Dimensional (2-D) Shapes

Poggo is learning all about shapes so he can make a monsterific shape picture and talk about the shapes he has used.
He knows the names of some shapes, but doesn't always get them right!

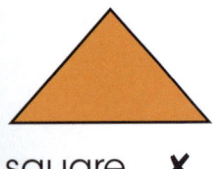  

square ✗   square ✓

1 Draw a line to match the shape name with the picture.

triangle

square

circle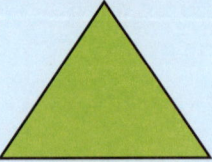

rectangle

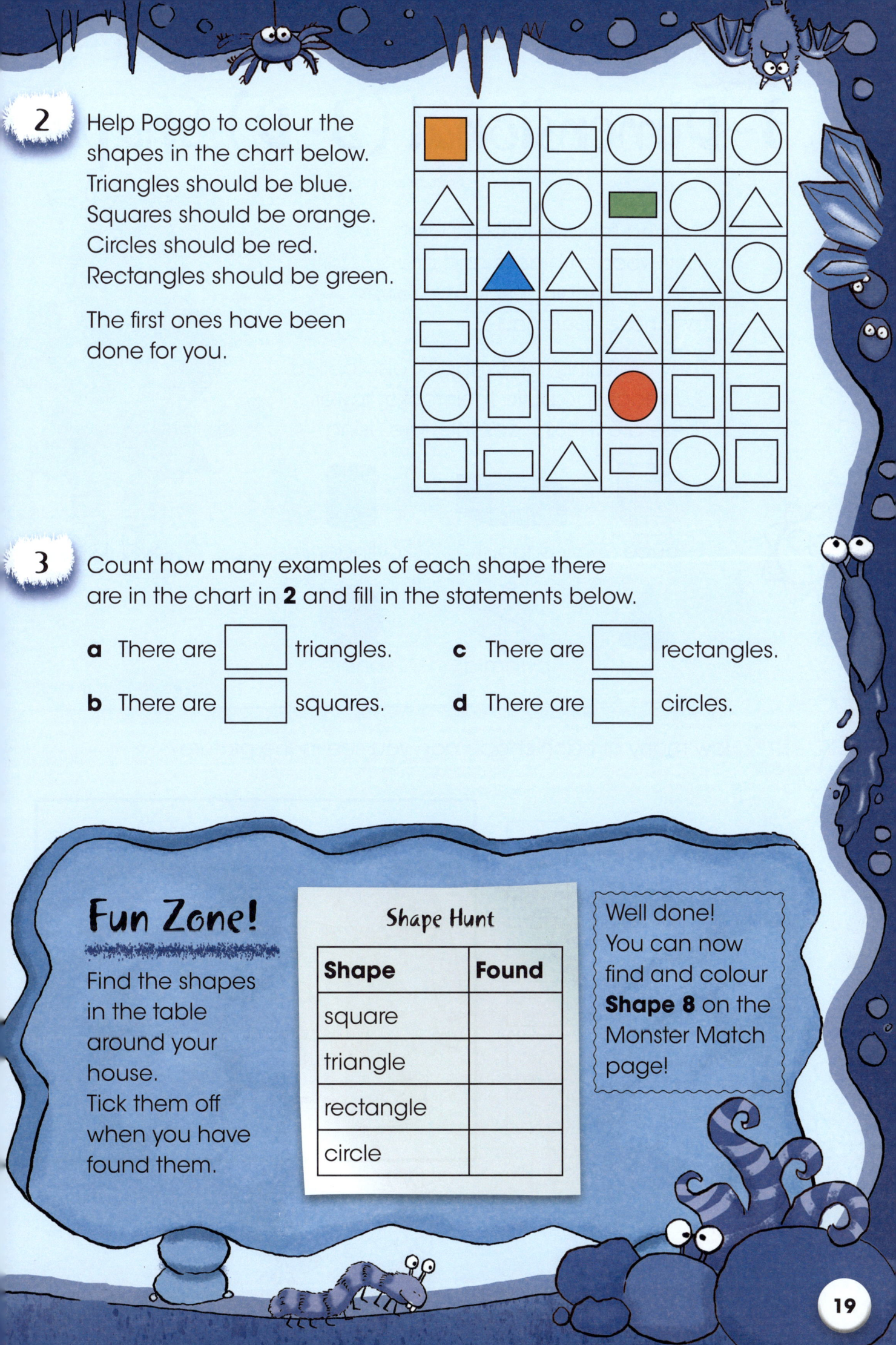

3-Dimensional (3-D) Shapes

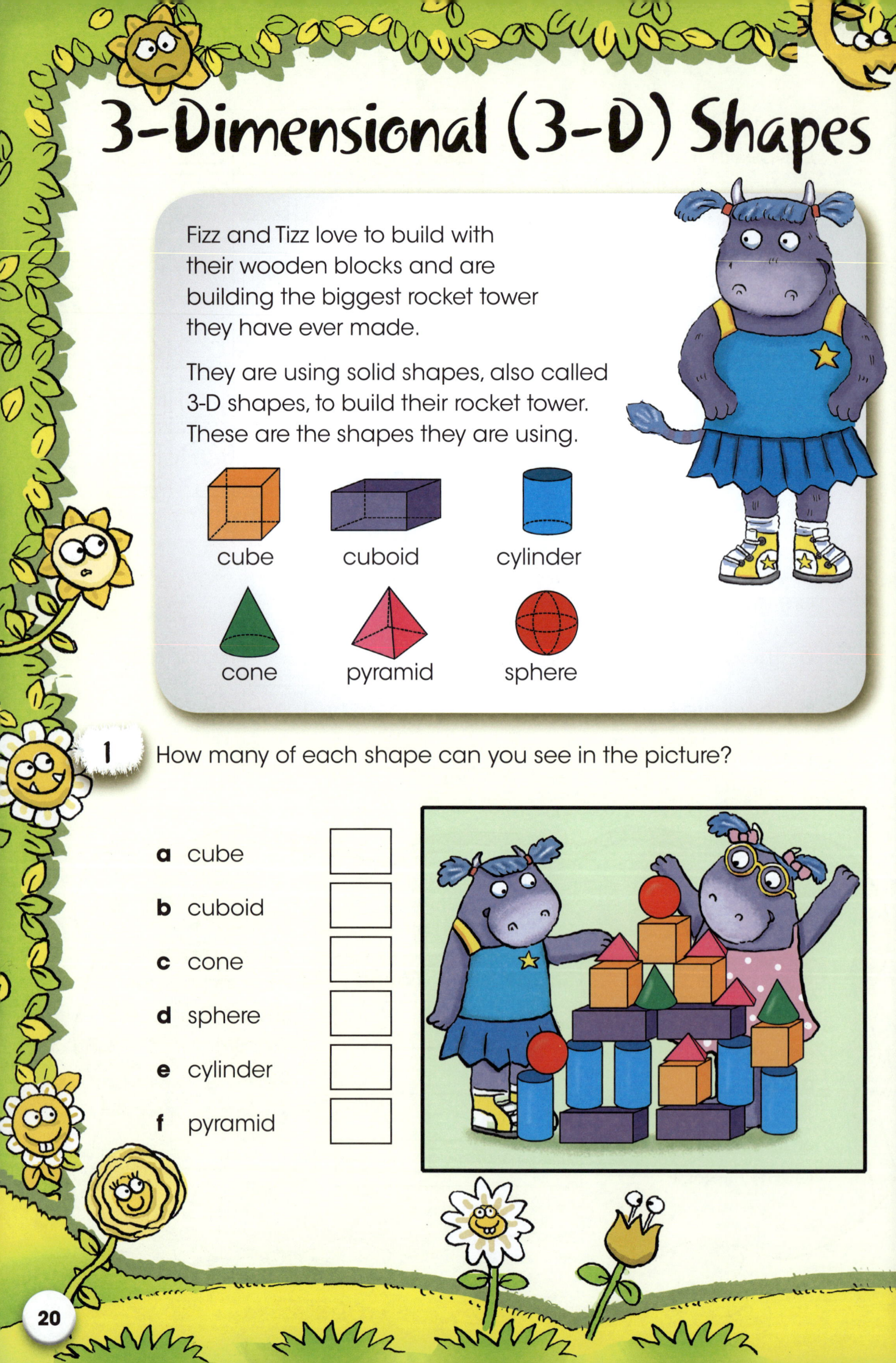

Fizz and Tizz love to build with their wooden blocks and are building the biggest rocket tower they have ever made.

They are using solid shapes, also called 3-D shapes, to build their rocket tower. These are the shapes they are using.

cube   cuboid   cylinder
cone   pyramid   sphere

1 How many of each shape can you see in the picture?

a cube
b cuboid
c cone
d sphere
e cylinder
f pyramid

2 Poggo has come to see the super rocket tower Fizz and Tizz have made. The monsters want to test your knowledge of 3-D shapes.
Each monster is giving you some clues about the shape that they are hiding.
Tick the correct shape that they are describing.

a It has a circle on the top and the bottom, and feels round in between.

b It feels completely round and smooth.

c It has a circle at one end, and a point on the other. It has a curved side.

Fun Zone!

Have fun making a rainbow suncatcher!

Well done! You can now find and colour Shape 9 on the Monster Match page!

Rainbow Suncatcher

You will need some transparent plastic sheet (e.g. from food packaging), food colouring, washing-up liquid, a paintbrush, PVA glue and cotton wool. Ask an adult to help when needed.

1 Use the paint to make a rainbow outline on the plastic sheet.
2 Place some glue in a dish, add 1–2 drops of washing-up liquid and mix.
3 Add 1–2 drops of food colouring, mix and paint your rainbow.
4 Leave it to dry.
5 Use some glue to attach some cotton wool to look like clouds at the ends of the rainbow.
6 Hang it up in your window, to brighten up your room!

Measuring

Poggo is building a new skateboarding ramp so needs to buy some wood. The price of wood depends on its **mass**. The mass of something is measured using scales, in **kilograms** (**kg**) and **grams** (**g**).
He will also need to measure how tall the ramp is.
The **height** of an object is usually measured in **metres** (**m**) and **centimetres** (**cm**).
Poggo and Dad go to the woodwork shop to buy the wood for the ramp. Dad says they should weigh the wood to find out which type will be the lightest to carry.
This cherry wood has a mass of 50 kg.

1 Look at the pictures of the scales, and write down how heavy the different types of wood are.

a cherry ☐ kg

b oak ☐ kg

c pine ☐ kg

d Write down which wood is the lightest. _____

2 Poggo likes his very tall ramp, because he can go very high on his skateboard. He asks Webber to help him put a special measuring stick called a **metre ruler** behind the ramp, so he can find out how high his jumps are. In this picture, Poggo's jump is 76 cm high.

Look at these pictures and write how high Poggo jumps.

a ☐ cm   b ☐ cm   c ☐ cm

Fun Zone!

Whether you are on the beach or in a sandpit or muddy garden, you can make a monster footprint!

Well done! You can now find and colour Shape 10 on the Monster Match page!

Monster Feet

You will need a clear space outside, either on a beach or in a sandpit at the park.

You can choose to either keep your shoes on or to take them off and have bare feet.

Ask an adult to help when needed.

1 Put your feet together and shuffle them about to make a big oval shape in the sand.
2 Next, dig one of your heels in front to make 4 toes. (Monsters only have 4 toes.)
3 Do a big jump to make the next monster footprint. Remember to land with your feet together!
4 Repeat until you have a series of giant feet printed in the sand.
5 It will look like a monster has walked by!

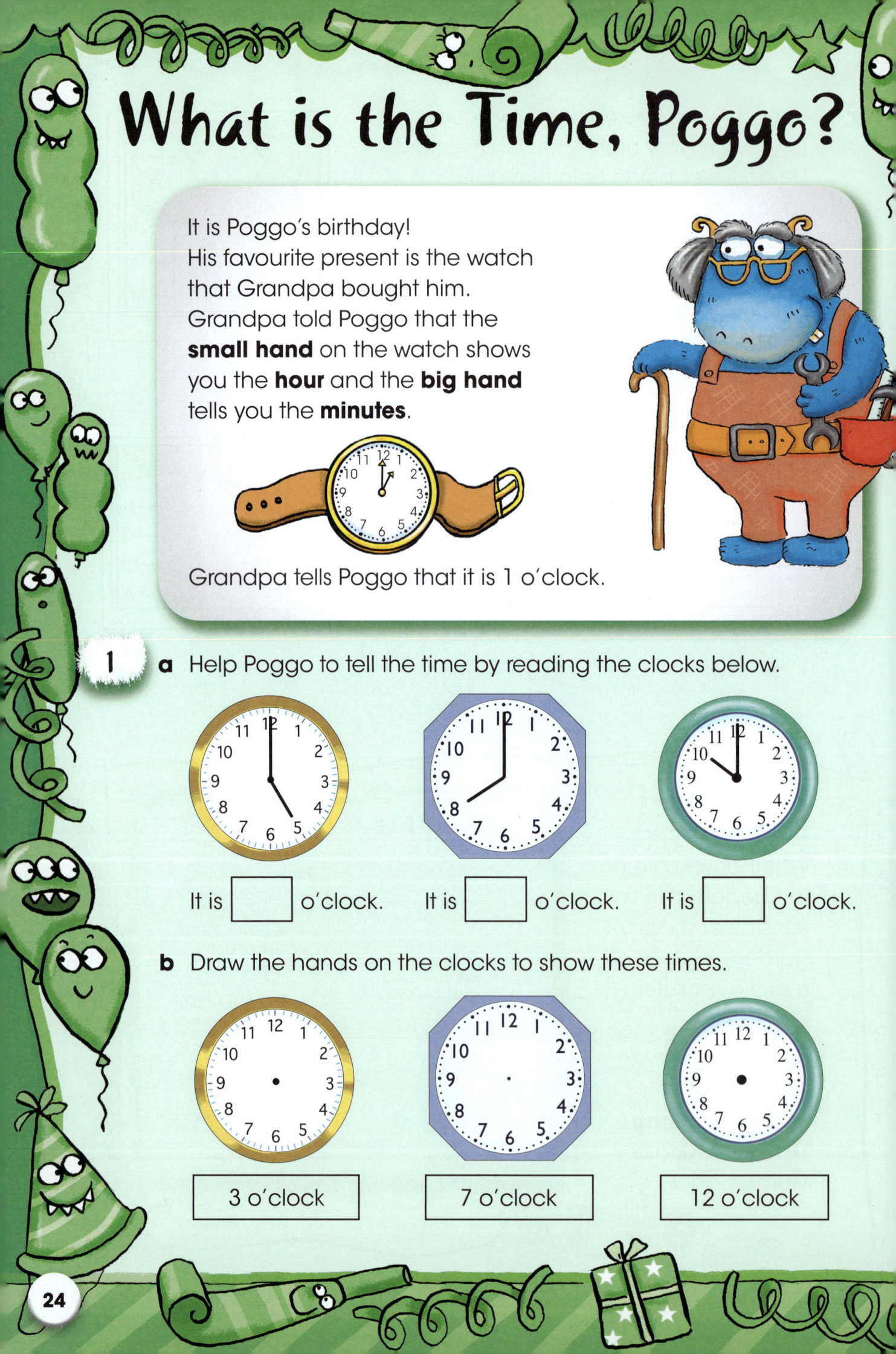

2 Litmus is in a muddle and cannot work out which things he needs to do first in the day. Help him start with the earliest and finish with the latest. Write a number in the box above each job to show the order.

☐ eating breakfast

☐ going to sleep

☐ getting dressed for school

☐ bedtime story

☐ going to school

Fun Zone!

Count how many skips you can do in 1 minute and record it in the table. Ask an adult to time you with a watch. See if you can beat your score tomorrow.

Day	Number of skips

Monsterific! You can now find and colour **Shape 11** on the Monster Match page!

Monster Challenge 2

1 Colour $\frac{1}{2}$ of these objects in.

a b c

2 Colour $\frac{1}{4}$ of these objects in.

a b c

3 Colour $\frac{3}{4}$ of these objects in.

a b c

4 Put each of the names of the shapes in the 2-D column or the 3-D column.

2-D shapes	3-D shapes

rectangle cone
cylinder circle
cuboid triangle
square pyramid
sphere cube

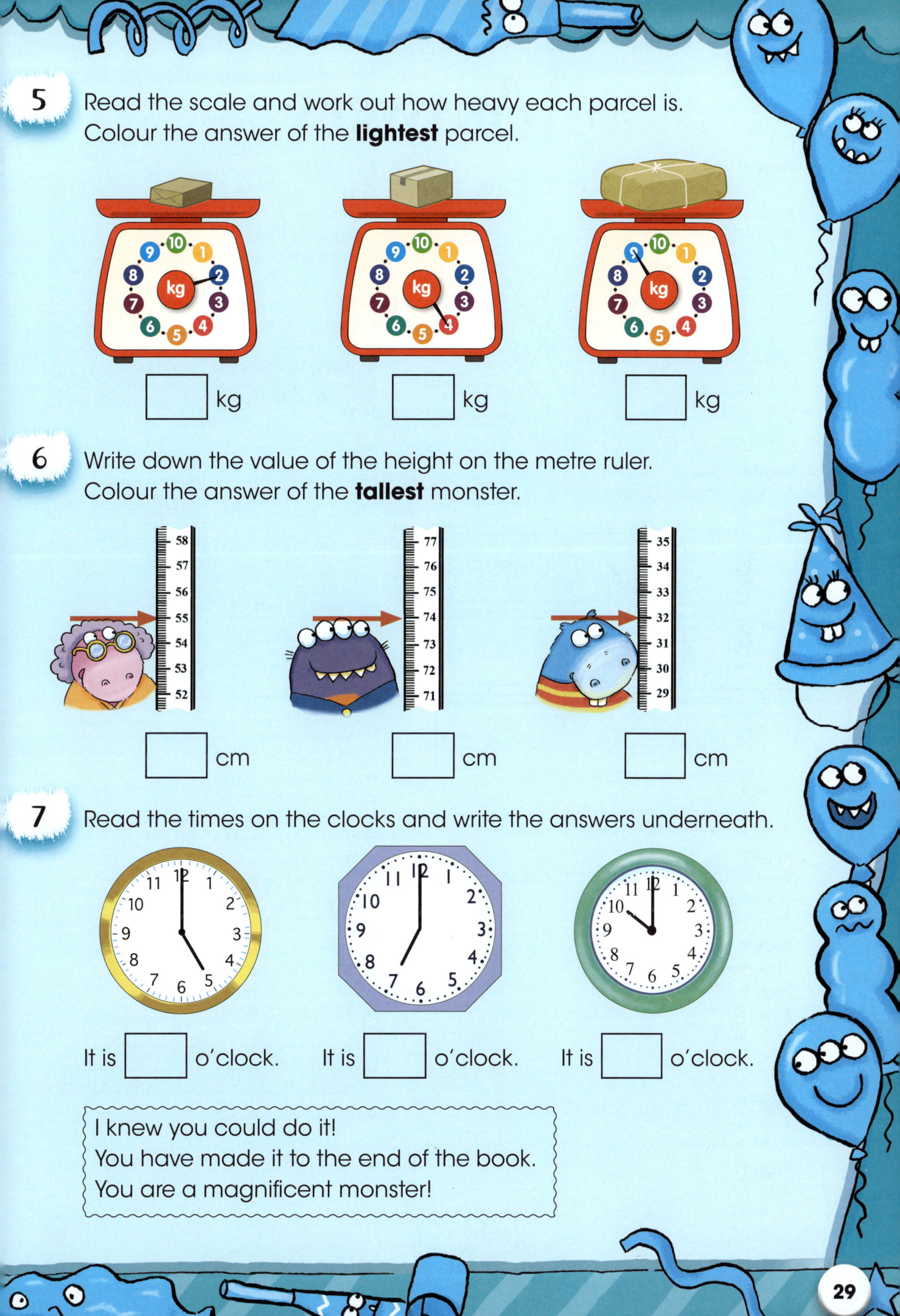

Answers

Page 2
1 Child to give verbal answers.

Page 3
2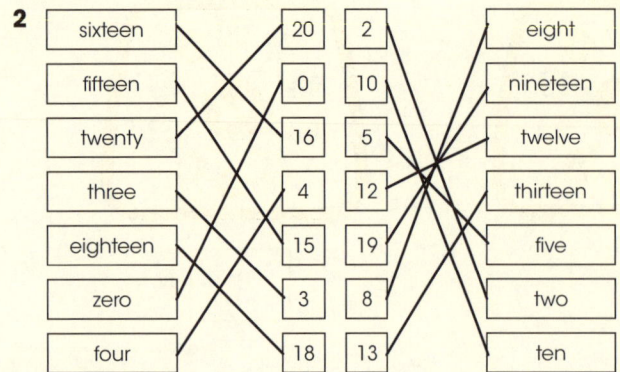

Page 4
1 a 32   b 70   c 69

Page 5
2 a
   b
   c

Page 6
1 32 should be circled.
2 68 should be circled.

Page 7
1 Monsters with numbers 7, 23, 11 and 59 should be coloured in.
2 Even

Page 8
1 a 9 + 4 = 13   b 8 + 12 = 20

Page 9
2 a 37   d 28
   b 32   e 41
   c 30   f 25
3 23 + 12 = 35

Page 10
1 a 8 – 3 = 5
   b 10 – 4 = 6

Page 11
2 a 17   d 12
   b 31   e 25
   c 16   f 30

Page 12
3 37 – 18 = 19

Page 12
1 a Each pair of gloves should be circled.
      Answer = 10
   b Each pair of gloves should be circled.
      Answer = 12

Page 13
2 a 25
   b 40
3 a Poggo and Fizz have 5 cards each.
   b Poggo and Fizz have 4 cards each.

Page 14
1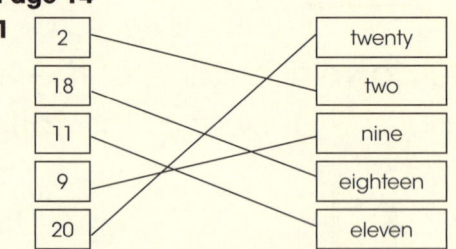

2

Number	Tens	Ones
43	4	3
12	1	2
98	9	8
76	7	6
57	5	7

3 a 24 should be circled.
   b 89 should be circled.
   c 99 should be circled.
   d 78 should be circled.
4 a 23 should be circled.
   b 5 should be circled.
   c 42 should be circled.
   d 12 should be circled.

Page 15
5 a 29   c 33
   b 50   d 44
6 a 42   c 16
   b 31   d 19
7

1	2	3	4	5	6	7	8	9	10
11	12	13	14	15	16	17	18	19	20

8 a 8   b 25
9   Fizz   Tizz
   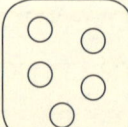 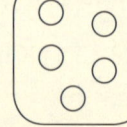

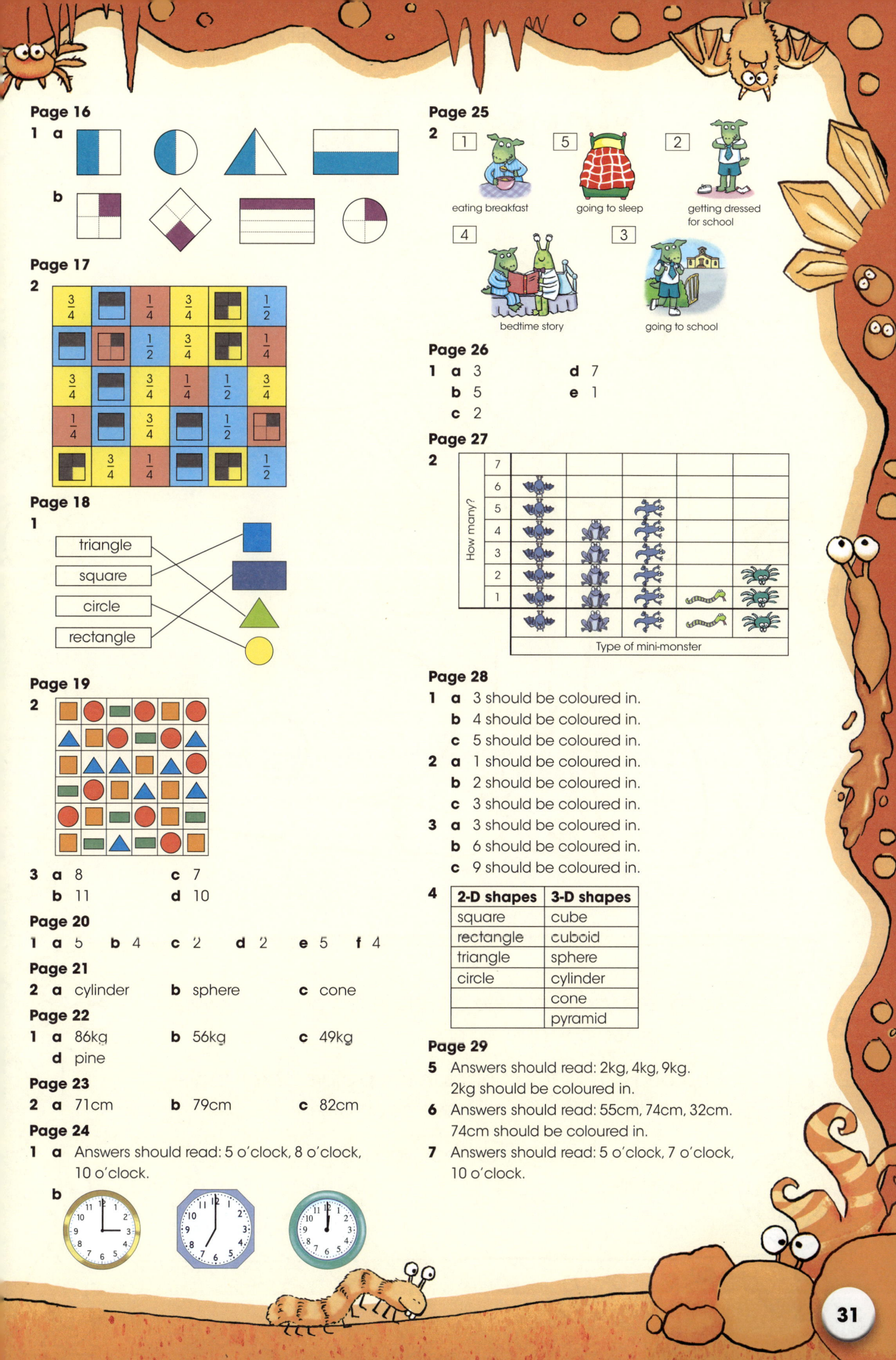

Monster Match

Each time you complete a topic in this book, you will be awarded a shape number.

Find and colour the shapes in the picture of Zak that match the numbers you have been given.

As you work through the book you will gradually see Zak come to life!